WHEELS
AND
WINGS

Exploring
the World of
Transportation
and Travel

VOCABUREADER
WORKBOOK 6

By Susannah J. Clark
and Raymond C. Clark

Illustrated by Maisie Crowther

PRO LINGUA **ASSOCIATES**

Brattleboro, Vermont

Published by Pro Lingua Associates
15 Elm Street
Brattleboro, Vermont 05301
802-257-7779
SAN 216-0579

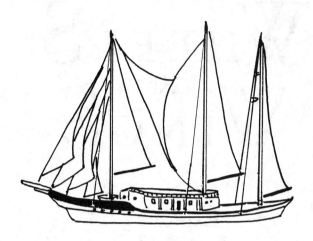

ISBN 0-86647-053-0

This book was set in the Caledonia or Highland typeface by Stevens
Graphics and printed and bound by The Book Press, both of
Brattleboro, Vermont. Designed by Arthur A. Burrows.

Printed in the United States of America.

Contents

INTRODUCTION

This book is a vocabulary development text focusing on words associated with travel and transportation. This special vocabulary is presented in thirteen readings with accompanying exercises. The passages are written in a redundant style so that you can learn the definition of each key word through the context. Although you may have to use a dictionary from time to time, you should try to understand the meaning of the word by studying the sentences and words which precede and follow the key word. In that way, you can develop both new vocabulary and good reading skills. The book is organized according to the following plan:

Illustration

Each reading has an illustration that helps you understand the vocabulary in the reading. Look at the picture before you read. The names for the parts of the picture are in the back of the book.

Reading

Each reading selection describes one aspect of the ways in which people move from one place to another. The key vocabulary is in **boldface**.

Exercises

Four exercises follow each reading selection. The exercises progress from easy to more difficult and require you to explore the forms and meaning of the key words. In the fourth exercise, the words are often used in a context that is not about moving. The exercises are not tests. They are teaching exercises, and it is expected you will make some mistakes. You can teach yourself by using the answers in the back of the book, but try to do the exercises first, before you check the answers.

Answers

The answers for all the exercises are found at the back of the book.

Illustration Key

The key for each illustration (picture) can be found here.

Key Word Index

This is an alphabetical list of all the key words and the number of the reading in which they appear.

1
Introductory Reading

Throughout history people have needed to **move** from one place to another. At first, we moved on foot, **walking** and **carrying** our things with us. Then we trained animals to **transport** both ourselves and our things. Then we used the sea and built boats, and we made wheels to move faster and carry more on land. In very recent history we invented engines to power our boats and wheeled **vehicles**. And finally, we learned how to **fly** — even to the moon.

Each technological advance brought us greater **mobility** and freedom, and this has changed our societies and ourselves. This is especially true in North America. When Europeans came to the Americas, they found a great continent that took months to cross. For example, in 1804-1806, the explorers Lewis and Clark **traveled** for 18 months, going more than 2000 miles from St. Louis, Missouri, on the Mississippi River to Portland, Oregon, on the Pacific Ocean. Today, that same **journey** takes about 40 hours by car and four hours by plane.

On the vast stage of the North American continent, the actors were a restless people who traveled across the land in search of independence, freedom, and prosperity. The drama was an incredible story of man's ability to move faster, farther, and easier. Fulton developed a steamboat (1807). A transcontinental railroad was completed (1869). The Wright Brothers flew (1903), and in 1913, Henry Ford put the continent on wheels with his Model T automobile.

Our world has been changed by our need to move.

Key words

move	transport	mobility
walk	vehicle	travel*
carry	fly	journey

* traveled can be spelled with two l's

I. Fill in the blanks with one of the key words above.

1. An automobile is a four-wheeled _____.

2. Birds and airplanes can _____.

3. A _____ of a thousand miles begins with a single step.

4. She got her ticket at a _____ agency.

5. _____ is the ability to _____.

6. I like to _____; it's good exercise.

7. Would you please _____ this suitcase for me?

8. _____ation is the act or means of carrying people or things from one place to another.

II. Choose the correct form of the words in parentheses.

1. Man has always (move, moved, moving) from one place to another.

2. He (journey, journeying, journeyed) day and night to reach his destination.

3. Let's take a (walked, walk, walking).

4. This (vehicle, vehicular) can (carried, carry, carrying) five people.

5. I like (fly, flying, flew) very much, but I have never (fly, flew, flown) a plane myself.

6. Marco Polo was one of history's most famous (travels, travelers, travel).

7. North Americans are a very (mobile, mobility) people.

8. Boats are still the cheapest way to (transport, transportation) some goods.

2

2
Walking

About two million years ago, humans began to walk and **run** on two legs. This ability to move from one place to another on two legs became very important in human social development. The location of the first human communities was determined by walking **distances**. Hunting grounds (a good place to catch animals for food) and a supply of water had to be located within 15 miles (24 km) of the community. This was the distance a person could walk to and from in one day.

Early societies were ruled by those who were the best walkers. The most powerful people could walk great distances **rapidly**, and they were the most successful at hunting. Because of the great importance of hunting, the best hunters became the first leaders.

Pedestrian man gradually spread across the entire planet as great **migrations** of people moved outward from Africa to populate other continents. The first great cities were built to serve the pedestrian. In Athens, the Acropolis was built to be visible from all **paths** in the city. Other cities built great elevated pathways for pedestrians so they would be above the animals and carts in the streets. Great empires like the Roman Empire were created by soldiers who walked as much as 21 miles a day to conquer Europe, North Africa, and the Middle East. Marco Polo walked and **rode** 25,000 miles on his **trip** from Italy to China in the late 13th century.

The basic measure of distance still used in America today is based on walking distances. The foot, the basic unit of this measurement system, was the length of a human foot. A yard (three feet) was the distance of a single **stride**, a long step. The

3

1

2

3

4

5

6

7

8

9

word "mile" originally meant a thousand **paces**, although a mile nowadays is actually 1760 yards (about 1.6 kilometers).

In recent history, we humans moved away from walking, the most independent means of travel, and began to ride animals and use animals to carry things. With the Industrial Revolution and the invention of the engine, we developed trains and boats to **cover** long distances, and then finally, in this century, automobiles and airplanes.

In the 1970s there was an energy crisis when the supply of oil and gas was reduced. People began to realize they were very dependent on their automobiles. At the same time, people became more health-conscious, and they realized the health benefits of walking, **jogging**, and bicycling. Soon, Americans were jogging in great numbers. Today, running shoes are one of the most popular items sold in shoestores.

In the 1980's, however, people began to return to walking for exercise. Many joggers, while improving their health, frequently suffered injuries to their knees and ankles as a result of jogging and running. Walkers receive the same health benefits as joggers but with much safer results. Nowadays, more than 50 million Americans are striding along country paths and city streets, using walking as a principal means of exercise.

Key words

run	migration	pace
distance	path	ride
rapid	trip	cover
pedestrian	stride	jog

I. Complete the definitions with a word from the list above.

1. _____ : Fast or quick.

2. To _____ : To go very rapidly on foot from one place to another.

3. To _____ : To go on an animal or in a vehicle.

4. The _____ : The amount of space between two points (It can be long or short).

5. To _____ : To move across the distance between two points.

6. A _____ : A long step or pace.

7. A _____ : The distance covered in one step, or the rate of movement of a walker or runner.

8. To _____ : To run at a slow pace.

9. A _____ : A movement from one place to another, especially by a traveler.

10. A _____ : A person who is walking.

11. A _____ : A small road used especially by pedestrians or animals.

12. A _____ : A group of people or animals moving from one place to another.

6

Verb (Present)	Verb (Past)	Verb (-ING Form)	Noun	Noun (Person)
run(s)	ran	running	**run**	runner
walk(s)	walked	walking	**walk(s)**	walker
ride(s)	rode	riding	**ride(s)**	rider
jog(s)	jogged	jogging	**jog**	jogger
pace(s)	paced	pacing	**pace(s)**	pacer
stride(s)	strode	striding	**stride(s)**	strider
cover(s)	covered	covering	—	—
migrate(s)	migrated	migrating	**migration(s)**	migrant

	Noun	Adjective	Adverb
	path(s)		
	trip(s)		
	pedestrian(s)	pedestrian	
	distance(s)	distant	distantly
	rapidity	rapid	rapidly

II. Use one of the word forms from the chart above in the sentences below:

1. Marco Polo (walk) _____ and (ride) _____ thousands of miles.

2. She is not (run) _____ anymore. She (jog) _____ instead.

3. Can you slow down? Your (pace) is _____ too fast.

4. We (cover) _____ 2,000 miles on our (trip) _____ to Hudson Bay last year.

5. They walked (rapid) _____ along the (path) _____.

6. Airplanes can (cover) _____ a great (distance) _____ very (rapid) _____.

7. He was (stride) _____ down the street yesterday.

8. This path is for (pedestrian) _____ and bicycles only.

7

III. Use the best word in these sentences. Use each word once.

1. The plane was _____ at 750 k.p.h.

2. The dog was _____ after the cat.

3. He stopped _____ when his knees began to hurt.

4. She was _____ slowly across the street.

5. He was _____ on a horse.

    a.   walking
    b.   jogging
    c.   moving
    d.   riding
    e.   running

❀ ❀ ❀ ❀ ❀

6. Nervously, she _____ the floor.

7. Confidently, he _____ across the hall.

8. Eventually, they _____ the entire distance.

9. Gradually, the first humans _____ northward.

    a.   paced
    b.   covered
    c.   strode
    d.   migrated

❀ ❀ ❀ ❀ ❀

10. _____ should cross the street here.

11. What is the _____ between here and Chicago?

12. At this point, the river moves more _____.

13. This road was originally just a narrow _____.

14. Last year they made their first _____ across the country.

    a.   rapidly
    b.   distance
    c.   path
    d.   trip
    e.   pedestrians

IV. Fill in the blanks with the correct form of one of the key words.

1. I'd like to make a long-_____ telephone call.

2. Don't cross here. The _____ crossing is at the corner.

3. He is the fastest _____ in our school.

4. Can you give me a _____ to work tomorrow?

5. The pedestrian walked _____ across the street.

6. I can't keep up this _____; I've got to slow down.

7. At noontime there are hundreds of _____ in Central Park.

8. There is a _____ from here to the river.

9. They like to take short _____ on the weekend.

10. Every fall thousands of Canada geese _____ southward.

11. The two runners matched each other _____ for
_____ throughout the entire race.

12. We're going to _____ a lot of ground in this course.

9

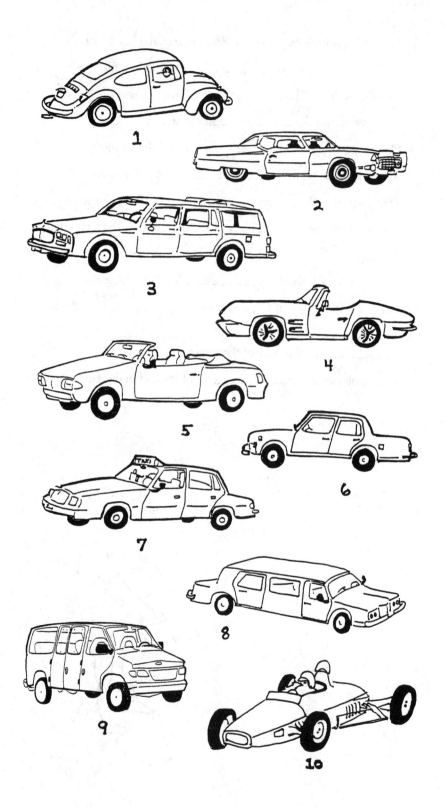

3
Automobiles

Automobiles are the principal means of transportation in the United States. There are more than 130 million **passenger** cars in the United States. Nine out of ten American adults have a **driver's** license. More than one third of the world's passenger cars are in the United States, and the United States contains more than four million miles (6.4 million km) of roads.

The Interstate Highway System was started in 1956 by the federal government. It was designed to provide safe, efficient four-lane highways throughout the states. Some interstate highways stretch for thousands of miles, crossing many states. The longest Interstate in the United States is Route 90, which **runs** 2,910 miles from Boston to Seattle, through 13 different states.

In the eastern United States, the important roads are often called highways. Some roads are **toll** roads. In other words, **motorists** must pay money to use the highway. Toll roads are often called turnpikes. In the West, highways are often called freeways, but not all of them are really free.

All American highways are numbered so travelers can identify them easily. Routes running east-west have even numbers (2, 4, 6, etc.), and north-south highways have odd numbers (1, 3, 5, etc.). City streets usually have names, the most common being Main Street. Some highways also have names, such as the Ventura Freeway in Los Angeles and the Lincoln Highway that runs from New York City to San Francisco.

Because of all the vehicles and highways, everyday life in the United States depends on the automobile. Most people would say their car is a necessity. They need it for work, shopping, visiting, and recreation.

Automobiles also create many problems. In the cities many **commuters** drive into the city every day to work. The large number of cars in the city streets often causes **traffic** jams, and the cars pollute the air, causing **smog**. During the morning and evening rush hours, when people are trying to enter or leave the city, the average car contains only 1.13 people. Some cities provide special lanes on the streets and highways for cars with more than one person.

Most **accidental** deaths in the United States are caused by motor vehicle accidents. In 1986, almost 50,000 people were killed and almost two million injured in traffic accidents. These numbers have been decreasing, however, because of an increased emphasis on **safety**. **Speed** limits are strictly enforced by the police. **Fines** for speeding can be expensive. And as of July 1988, 32 states had laws requiring automobile passengers to wear **seat belt**s.

American society depends on the automobile and the automobile depends on gasoline. There will be great changes in the United States, and in the world, when the supply of gasoline is gone.

Key words

passenger	drive	safety	commuter
toll	traffic	speed	
motorist	smog	fine	
run	accident	seat belt	

I. Use one of the key words above in the sentences below.

1. A combination of smoke and fog is _____, which is a form of air pollution.

2. The money you pay for using a highway is a _____, and the money you pay for breaking a law is a _____.

3. The act of using a car is called _____ing.

4. A person who drives a motor car is a _____.
A person who is not driving the car is a _____.
A person who drives to and from work each day is a _____.

5. If you don't drive carefully, you may have an _____.

6. Driving too fast is going beyond the _____ limit.

7. An important _____ rule is: Don't speed. Another one is: Wear your _____. When the _____ is heavy, be especially careful. Drive safely.

8. The act of moving very fast on foot is called _____ing. If a car's motor is going, it is also _____ing. And a highway that goes from Detroit to Boston _____s for 800 miles from Detroit to Boston.

II. Choose the correct form of the word in parentheses.

1. Attention (motors, motorists, motorers)! This road is closed.

2. This is the last exit before the (toll, tolling, tolls) road.

3. State law: All (passenger, passengers) must wear a (seat, seating, seat's) belt.

4. There is a heavy (fine, find, fines) for (speed, speeding, speeds) in this state.

13

5. Avoid (accidentals, accidents). Drive (safety, safely).

6. It's another (smog, smoggy) day in L.A.

7. This route (running, runs, run) north and south.

8. The (traffic, trafficking) is very heavy today.

9. In England people (drivers, drive, driving) on the left.

10. She (commute, commutes, commuter) from the suburbs to the city every day.

III. Use the correct form of one of the key words in the sentences and signs below.

1. The car was not moving, but its _____ was _____.

2. In this state _____ in the back seat do not have to wear a _____.

3. The accident caused a huge _____ jam.

4. I have _____ between Boston and Newburyport for 25 years.

5. Some days the _____ is so bad it hurts my eyes.

6.
CAUTION !
PAY _____ AHEAD
LANES 1 AND 2
FOR _____
WITH CORRECT CHANGE
THE _____ IS $1.00

7.
_____ **KILLS!**
**OBSERVE
THE**
_____
LIMIT

14

8.
```
S_____
  IS NO
A_____
```

9.
```
THE _____ IN
 THIS STATE
     FOR
  DRINKING
WHILE _____
  IS $500
```

IV. Use one of the key words in these sentences.

1. A _____ train carries _____ to and from the city Monday through Friday. It is very fast. It can reach a _____ of 75 miles per hour.

2. There is often no _____ on a freeway; it is _____ -free. Free telephone calls are also called _____ -free calls.

3. Outside the city, the air is usually _____ -free.

4. Red, yellow, and green lights are _____ signals.

5. In 1986 there were 94,000 _____ deaths in the United States. 48,700 of the deaths were caused in _____ vehicle _____ .

6. The Nile River _____ north and south.

7. She is a very _____ driver. She has never had an _____ . She has a perfect _____ record. And she has never paid a traffic _____ .

8. When the no smoking and _____ _____ signs are turned off, _____ may smoke and leave their _____ .

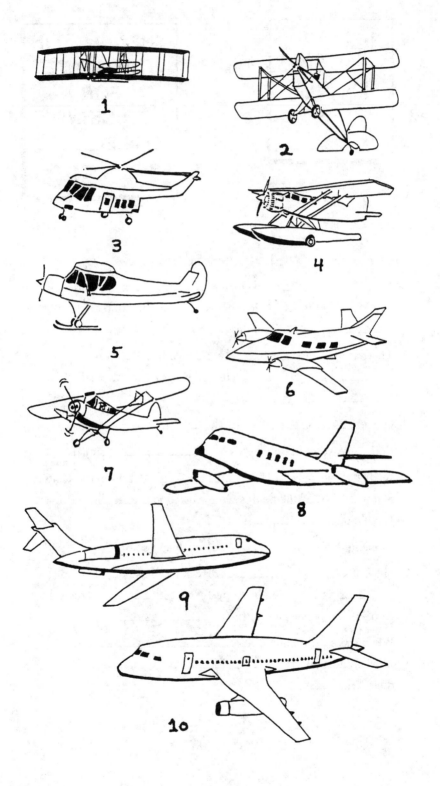

4
Domestic Airlines

Most people know that the first power-driven **flight** was made at Kitty Hawk, North Carolina, by Orville Wright. On December 17, 1903, Orville flew the Flyer I for 12 seconds at an **altitude** averaging ten feet above the ground while his brother Wilbur looked on.

Today over five million people make domestic flights in the United States every year. These flights can be from fewer than ten to several thousand miles long. The shortest domestic flight runs seven miles from Bethel to Napaiskak in Alaska and takes only ten minutes. The longest flights run from coast to coast, and can **last** as much as six hours.

On a **round trip** across the country, the flight west takes longer to complete than flying east. This is because the jet stream, the wind which flows across the United States from west to east, slows down flights going west and at the same time speeds up flights going east. As a result, **nonstop** flights **heading** west can take more than six hours while a flight east lasts only about five hours.

Although there are more than 12,000 civilian airports in the United States, fewer than 1,000 of these are big enough for an airplane that can carry 20 or more passengers. More than three-fourths of all planes in America are single-engine planes that can carry only a few people. Including these small planes, in 1987 Americans made almost 450 million flights.

Americans fly for many reasons. People on vacation sometimes take a plane to their **destination**. Students who attend a university far away from their homes often fly home for Christmas and summer breaks. However, most of the passengers on airlines today are making business trips.

Upon reaching the airport, travelers must **check in** at the check-in counter to receive a **boarding pass** that tells the row and number of their seat. They are also given the number of the **gate** their plane is leaving from. On international flights, if the plane has both a smoking and a non-smoking section, travelers are also asked which they prefer to travel in. Nowadays, there is no smoking on domestic flights, and some airlines do not permit smoking on any flights. Travelers may also check their luggage at the check-in counter. Some passengers who travel light are able to bring their bags with them on the plane as carry-on baggage. Passengers are not permitted to bring more than two bags with them into the plane.

When they board the plane, passengers are greeted by flight **attendants**, who help them locate their seats. If the flight lasts longer than an hour, flight attendants offer soft drinks or cocktails and serve snacks or a meal.

Most flights lasting longer than a few hours include an intermediate stop, sometimes called a stopover or layover. The stop lasts about an hour. Travelers sometimes change planes during a layover. But even if they do not have to change planes, travelers are usually allowed to **disembark** in order to stretch their legs or buy a book at the airport shops.

Key words

flight	nonstop	boarding pass
altitude	heading	gate
last	destination	attendant
round trip	check in	disembark

I. Use the key words above in the following sentences.

1. The place you are going to is your _____.

2. A trip in a plane is called a _____.

3. To go to a place and come back is called a _____ _____ flight. A flight with no return is a one-way flight.

4. A flight with no layovers is a _____ flight.

5. When you come to the airport, first you go to the _____ counter to _____.

6. We will be flying at an _____ of 40,000 feet.

7. The place where you get on or off a plane is a _____.

8. You need a _____ _____ to _____ (get on) the plane.

9. A _____ _____ can help you find your seat on the plane.

10. When you arrive at your destination, you _____.

11. A flight across the country will _____ about five or six hours, depending on which way you are going.

12. If your flight is _____ east it takes less time.

19

II. Match the following words with a definition.

1. flight	1. _____	a. to report for a flight
2. to last	2. _____	b. someone who helps
3. round trip	3. _____	c. the height above the ground
4. nonstop	4. _____	d. to get on the plane
5. to head	5. _____	e. to continue in time
6. destination	6. _____	f. the place to enter or leave
7. to check in	7. _____	g. to go in a certain direction
8. to board	8. _____	h. an airplane trip
9. gate	9. _____	i. to get off the plane
10. attendant	10. _____	j. with no layovers
11. altitude	11. _____	k. a journey to and from
12. to disembark	12. _____	l. the end of a trip

III. Use a key word to complete this conversation.

Announcement: _____ 103 from San Diego is arriving at _____ 32.

A. Welcome back! How was your _____?

B. It was long. We had stopovers in Denver and Chicago.

A. How long did the stopovers _____?

B. About one hour in each place.

A. Couldn't you fly _____?

B. No, all flights to this _____ have stops.

A. Did you _____ during the stops?

B. No, I stayed on the plane. But I had a nice conversation with one of the _____ _____.

A. That's nice. Was he handsome?

B. Very. But married.

20

A. So what time did you leave San Diego?

B. I _____ _____ at 10 a.m., but we didn't actually _____ until noon.

A. What was the delay?

B. All flights _____ east were delayed _____ by bad weather, I think.

A. So let's go get your luggage.

B. Ok, but after, I want to check on return flights. I didn't buy a _____ _____ ticket.

IV. Complete the following using a key word.

1. Will passenger J.P. Moran please report to the Atlantic Airlines _____ counter.

2. _____ 703 to Miami is now ready for _____ at _____ 22B. Please have your _____ _____ ready to give to the _____.

3. Good morning, this is your captain speaking. On this morning's _____ to Philadelphia we will be _____ west over the Grand Canyon. Our cruising _____ will be 35,000 feet. Our _____ to our intermediate stopover in St. Louis will _____ 3 hours and 10 minutes. For those of you whose final _____ is Philadelphia, the weather there is excellent. If you wish, you may _____ in St. Louis. Our stopover will _____ one hour.

4.

21

5
Railroads

Railroads are a good **way** to transport large amounts of material at low cost. Railroads are efficient because the friction between the **wheels** and the **rails** is very low. If a 40-ton train is **rolling** along a railroad **track** at 60 miles per hour and the engineer cuts the power, it will roll for five miles before coming to a stop. A train's low friction enables a locomotive to **haul** a long **line** of railroad cars very efficiently.

The first railroads were developed in Europe (especially in Great Britain) in the early 19th century. During the 1840's and 1850's, railroads became very important in North America. Most of these railroads were local lines, however, and did not go a long way. But gradually these local lines were **linked** together into larger systems. Chicago became an important city because it was at the **junction** of many railroad lines.

During the middle of the 19th century, two companies began to build America's first transcontinental railroad. The two companies, the Union Pacific and the Central Pacific, began a race to see who could build the most track. On May 10, 1869, the two railroads met at Promontory Point, Utah, linking the two coasts of the continent.

Railroads continued to grow in the late 19th and early 20th centuries. In 1886 the Trans-Canada line was completed, linking Halifax, Nova Scotia, and Vancouver, British Columbia. In 1916 the world's longest railroad, the Trans-Siberian Railroad, was completed. It covers a distance of 5,787 miles from Moscow to Vladivostok.

In the 20th century the importance of railroads decreased, especially in the United States. Although the railroads continue to haul **freight**, the number of passenger trains has decreased. Today the most successful passenger trains cover short-distance runs. Many of them bring commuters to large metropolitan areas like New York City.

Nowadays, long-distance train trips are not very common. Train **fare** is sometimes more expensive than airfare, and trains do not **depart** as often as airplanes do. A train takes three days to travel across the United States, while a plane covers the same distance in six hours or less. But some people still prefer to take the train. Some people are afraid of flying. Some like to see the scenery, and a trip across the continent on the Trans-Canada is an unforgettable experience. For many people it is still very exciting to board a train as the conductor walks down the **platform** calling, "All aboard!"

Key Words

way	track	junction	platform
wheel	haul	freight	
rail	line	fare	
roll	link	depart	

I. Use one of the key words above for each of the phrases below.)

1. _____ (to leave)

2. _____ (it's round and it rolls)

3. _____ (a method; a distance; a route)

4. _____ (the price for a ticket)

5. _____ (to connect; a connection)

6. _____ (to move along the road, especially like a wheel)

7. _____ (an intersection; a place where roads come together)

8. _____ (the place where passengers board the train)

9. _____ (to pull something)

10. _____ (things in a row; a transportation system)

11. _____ (material that is carried by a train)

12. _____ (the iron part of a railroad track)

13. _____ (the roadway that a train uses)

II. Circle the correct form of the word in these sentences.

1. There are three (way, ways, away) to get there.

2. A tricycle is a three-(wheeling, wheels, wheeled) vehicle.

3. A train rides on two parallel (rail, rails, railing).

4. The fast freight was (rolling, rolls, rolled) along at 100 k.p.h.

5. There are two (trackings, tracked, tracks) at this railroad crossing.

6. Millions of tons of freight were (hauling, haul, hauled) by the old Baltimore and Ohio (line, lining, lined).

7. The new route which (links, linked, linking) the two cities will be opened next month.

8. Do you know the old song "(Freights, Freight, Freighted) Train?"

9. Next week all the (fare, farings, fares) will increase.

10. The Pacific Flyer will (depart, departing, departure) at 11:45.

III. Choose the best word to complete the sentence.

1. There must be another _____ to go.

2. She was waiting on _____ B.

3. This place used to be an important _____.

4. There is a long _____ of autos waiting for the train to pass.

a. platform
b. junction
c. way
d. line

✻ ✻ ✻ ✻ ✻ ✻

5. This engine only hauls _____.

6 Our _____ has been delayed until 10 p.m.

7. The first-class is _____ 50% higher.

8. The _____ is perfectly straight for the next 10 miles.

a. departure
b. track
c. fare
d. freight

✻ ✻ ✻ ✻ ✻ ✻

9. They are opening a new _____ between the port and the interior.

10. A river, like a wheel, can _____.

11. The wheels came off the _____.
(The car was de_____ed.)

12. She lost a _____ on her luggage cart.

13. We can rent a U-_____ truck and move all our things to our new home.

a. wheel
b. rail
c. Haul
d. roll
e. link

26

IV. Fill in the blank with the correct form of one of the key words.

1. He fell off the _____ and hurt his leg.

2. Pittsburgh is at the _____ of the Allegheny and Monongahela Rivers.

3. Although hotel rates have not increased, the _____ for airline tickets have.

4. It's a long _____ to Tipperary.

5. Old Man River just keeps _____ along.

6. The opposite of arrival is _____ .

7. The Rock Island _____ is a mighty good railroad.

8. There's a missing _____ in this chain of events.

9. In the old days, sailors used to sing as they _____ on the ropes to raise the sails.

10. The path followed by runners is also called a _____.

11. For years he wandered around the country, riding the _____, traveling from place to place on _____ trains.
He often said he should have been born with _____, instead of legs.

1

2

3

4

5

6
Buses

Although vehicles have been used as buses for many years, it was not until 1922 that a company in Oakland, California, built the first vehicle specially designed to be a bus. By 1985, there were almost 80,000 buses in the United States, carrying more than six billion passengers a year.

Intercity buses are usually the least expensive type of long-distance public transportation. Intercity buses **pick up** passengers at a bus **terminal** where passengers buy their tickets. Travelers can put their **luggage** in the large **storage** spaces under the bus seats. Passengers can also keep smaller items in **racks** above the seats. Passengers show their ticket to the driver when they **get on** the bus.

Intercity buses do not make many **stops**. They usually make only one stop in each town and do not stop at every town along their **route**. On long trips without scheduled stops along the way, buses stop every few hours to allow passengers to **get off** and stretch their legs or get something to eat.

City buses carry people to destinations within city limits or to nearby suburbs. The fare for these trips is usually less than a dollar. City buses run a route of several miles. Some routes are very large circles, and the bus simply drives that route over and over all day. The buses operate on a schedule, so passengers will know when the next bus will arrive. Some popular routes are run very **frequently**, as often as every ten minutes. Some routes do not have many passengers and run only a few times a day.

Bus stops usually occur once a block. A bus stop is sometimes only a sign at the side of the road. Sometimes a stop will have a bench for passengers to sit on while they wait for the bus. Some stops even have small shelters for passengers to sit under when it rains or snows.

Bus drivers only stop at a bus stop if they see passengers waiting at the stop, or if the passengers on the bus signal that they wish to get off. In order to get off, passengers pull a cord that runs along the side of the bus. This cord is connected to a sign that lights up or a bell. The bus driver stops at the next bus stop when the cord is pulled. Sometimes passengers who are not familiar with the bus route do not know which stop is theirs. Bus drivers are usually very helpful. If passengers ask for help, the bus driver will tell them when the bus has reached their stop.

Passengers pay the fare when they get on the bus. Next to the driver's seat there is a box for the passengers to put their money into. Some of these boxes will take dollar bills, but bus drivers usually do not give change. People who often take the bus can buy bus **passes**. These passes are good for different lengths of time, usually between one and three months. When the passengers **get on** the bus, they show the driver their pass instead of paying the fare.

School buses are yellow buses that are only allowed to bring children to and from the school. Special traffic laws help protect school buses and their young passengers. Cars are not allowed to **pass** a stopped school bus. When the school bus stops to pick up or **drop off** children, other vehicles must also stop, even if they are approaching the bus from the opposite direction.

Sometimes groups of people will **charter** a bus for a special trip or a tour. Chartered buses do not pick up or **discharge** other people along their routes.

Some people do not like to make trips on buses. Long bus trips take more time than trips by train or airplane. But since buses are the least expensive way to travel, they are still very popular.

Key Words

pick up	rack	frequent
terminal	get on	pass
luggage	stop	drop off
storage	route	charter
	get off	discharge

I. Use the key words above in the blank spaces below.

1. When you enter a bus, you get _____. When you leave
   you get _____. But you get in and out of a car.

2. When the bus stops for you, it _____s you
   _____. When it stops to allow you to get off, it
   _____s you _____, or _____s you.

3. At a bus _____, intercity buses arrive and depart. At a bus
   _____ city buses pick up and drop off passengers. Both
   buses travel over regular _____s on a regular schedule. A
   city bus makes _____ stops. Intercity buses do not stop as
   _____ly as city buses. The frequency of arrivals and
   departures is shown on a schedule.

4. A _____ed bus is not a scheduled bus. It is a special bus,
   for a special trip. Airplanes are often _____ed by tourist
   agencies.

5. A ticket that can be used several times is often called a
   _____. This word can also mean to move past another
   vehicle, or to _____. As time goes by, it also
   _____es.

6. A large vehicle usually has a _____ space for suitcases so
   that passengers can store their _____. The space over the
   seat is called a _____. It's a good place to put a small
   package, but it's usually too small for big suitcases.

II. Rewrite the scrambled sentences below in the proper word order.

1. luggage My terminal the at is.

_____.

2. route we shall take Which?

_____.

3. vehicle stops This frequently.

_____.

4. bus discharged The has passengers its all.

_____.

5. He on bus the got.

_____.

6. in Dallas off She the bus got.

_____.

7. 9 a.m. him up We picked at.

_____.

8. her 11 a.m. at off We dropped.

_____.

9. stopped school bus pass Do not a.

_____.

10. overhead packages your Please store rack in the.

_____.

32

III. Can you use all the key words in this puzzle?
Here are some of them.

1. To unload.
2. To leave behind.
3. A place to store something.
4. The end; final.

5. To board.
6. To hire or lease a bus or plane.
7. A word on a sign.
8. The opposite of 5, above.

Now can you complete the puzzle and give a brief definition of the other key words?

9. - - - - - - - - : _____
10. - - - - - - : _____
11. - - - - - - - : _____
12. - - - - - : _____
13. - - - - - - - : _____
14. - - - - : _____

33

IV. Use the key words in the spaces below:

Dear Nancy,

It was great to see you again, and thanks again
for _____ me _____ at the Trans-
Continental Bus _____. It would have been difficult to _____ _____ and _____ the
city bus, and get to the _____ on time, with all
my _____. However, I was late anyway, and I
missed the 8 o'clock bus. Fortunately, the buses to Calgary
are fairly _____ — the next one was at 9:30 — so
I put my suitcases in a _____ locker and went
across the street for some breakfast.

The trip was reasonably comfortable. It wasn't really a
very scenic _____, but there were only two
_____ so the time _____ quickly.
Unfortunately, the lunch _____ was a disaster.
Just as our bus pulled up at Johnson Howard's Restaurant, a big _____ bus _____ about 60
passengers. I had to fight to get a hamburger.

My friend Albert _____ me _____ at
the Calgary station, and so here I am in Canada!

Love, *Kathy*

P.S. I think I left my umbrella on the bus, probably in the
overhead _____. But maybe I left it at your
house. If you find it, it's yours.

7

Boats

Boats are not widely used for passenger travel in the United States, but they still carry large quantities of **cargo**, both domestic and international. About 15 percent of all domestic cargo is still **shipped** by boat, mainly on the continent's two largest inland waterways: The Mississippi River System and the Great Lakes System. River barges on the Mississippi and ocean-going vessels on the Great Lakes and the St. Lawrence Seaway are still a common sight in the United States and Canada.

In the early history of the continent, boats were essential to the explorers and settlers because the land contained many large rivers and lakes. Native Americans and early explorers traveled by **paddling** their canoes on the inland waterways.

To **cross** the rivers, the early settlers used **ferries**. The first ferries were simple boats **propelled** by oars or poles. Sometimes ferries used **sails** to catch the wind and help them cross.

In 1790 John Fitch **operated** a ferry boat with a paddle wheel driven by a steam engine on the Delaware River. The paddle wheel boat become the model for the steamboats of the Mississippi River. The great river, however, was hazardous and difficult to **navigate**, but in 1816 Henry Miller Shreve **launched** a flat-bottomed paddle wheel steamboat that dominated the river traffic from 1820 to 1870.

The Mississippi River steamboats, carrying cotton and sugar helped New Orleans become a major **port**. Even today, it is the country's second largest port after New York City.

In the east, the Erie Canal was completed in 1825. It connected New York City with the Great Lakes and helped make

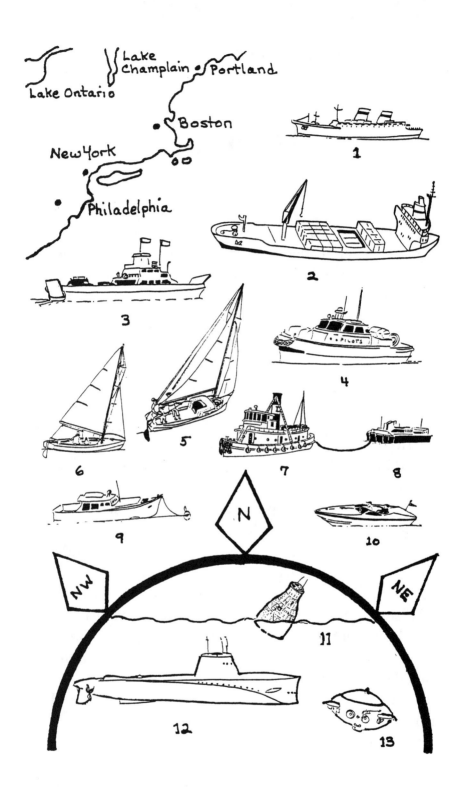

Lake Ontario

Lake Champlain • Portland

Boston

New York

Philadelphia

1

2

3

4

5

6

7

8

9

N

10

NW

11

NE

12

13

New York the United States' most important port. Large numbers of settlers and goods moved from the east coast to the country's interior. For many miles, from Albany to Buffalo, the canal barges were **towed** by mules, walking along the bank. Needless to say, this was not a fast way to go west.

In the 1850s, however, the river boats began losing trade to the railroads, and by the end of the 19th century the railroad had replaced the boats as the most important form of inland transportation.

Today, ferries still operate in many places. They have become popular again in cities where automobile traffic is heavy. Many commuters in San Francisco and New York prefer to take the ferry to work because it is quieter and more enjoyable. And although bridges now have reduced the need for ferries, there are still many interesting ferry rides in North America, such as the ferry in San Francisco Bay to Alcatraz prison, or the international ferry from Portland, Maine, to Yarmouth, Nova Scotia.

In the United States today, boats play a minor role in comparison with motor vehicles, trains and planes. But they still have three very special roles. First , merchant shipping is still essential to the international shipment of goods. Second, canoes, motorboats and sailboats are very popular for recreation. And finally they still have a place in the tourist industry, from **cruise** ships taking passengers on cruises to romantic vacation places, to the ferry that brings visitors from Manhattan Island in New York City to the Statue of Liberty.

Key Words

cargo	ferry	navigate
ship	propel	launch
paddle	sail	port
cross	operate	tow
		cruise

I. Use the key words to complete these definitions.

1. _____: A kind of boat that crosses from one side of a river to the other.

2. _____: It is used to propel a canoe.

3. _____: A tourist trip on a ship.

4. _____: A place that ships arrive at and depart from.

5. _____: Goods carried by a boat.

6. _____: To go from one side to another.

7. _____: To send goods from one place to another.

8. _____: To put a boat into the water - particularly for the first time.

9. _____: To move or push something forward.

10. _____: To use a vehicle or machine.

11. _____: To travel on water.

12. _____: To pull something

13. _____: To operate a boat by using the wind.

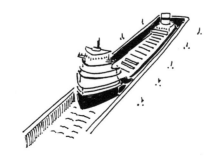

II. Choose the correct form of the words in parentheses.

1. (operate, operated, operation). He _____ a ferry.

2. (ship, shipped, shipment). We're expecting a new _____ of goods tomorrow.

3. (cross, crossed, crossing). In 1819 the steam and sail-powered ship Savannah _____ the Atlantic in 29 days.

4. (launch, launched, launching) The famous sailing ship Old Ironsides was _____ in Boston in 1797.

5. (Navigate, Navigated, Navigation) _____ on the Mississippi was not easy.

6. (propel, propelled, propellers) A motorboat is _____ by _____.

7. (cruise, cruised, cruising) For our vacation, we took a _____ ship to the Bahamas.

8. (ferry, ferried, ferrying) This old _____ has _____ passengers to the island for more than 50 years.

9. (paddle, paddled, paddling) He had to stop _____ because he broke his _____.

10. (sail, sailed, sailing) We went _____ on our new _____ boat.

11. (tow, towed, towing) The disabled ship was _____ into port by a _____ boat.

III. Use the correct form of a key word in these sentences.

Portsmouth used to be a very famous p_____. S_____ s_____ from all over the world used to come up the Piscataqua River to the docks. They brought c_____ of sugar, tea and spice. The river has a very strong current, however, and s_____ had to be t_____ from the mouth of the river by t_____ boats. The current is so strong, it is almost impossible to p_____ a canoe against it. Before the bridges were built, connecting New Hampshire and Maine, f_____ used to o_____ at several places. That was the only way to c_____ the treacherous river. The f_____ boat o_____ors had to be skillful n_____ors because they used only wind, oars and the current to p_____ their boats. During World War II many submarines were L_____ from the naval shipyard. Today, most of the boats on the river are pleasure boats and fishing boats. The only passenger service is a short, one-day c_____ to the Isles of Shoals, ten miles from the p_____ itself.

IV. Use one of the key words in these sentences.
Use each key word only once.

1. Flying Elephants Airlines doesn't carry passengers. It carries only _____.

2. We will _____ these goods by the fastest possible way.

3. This city doesn't have an air _____.

4. During the war, C-47s _____ thousands of tons of cargo into China from India. Powered by only two engines and two _____, it was very dangerous to _____ the Himalayas. The aircraft's pilot and _____ had to be very skillful.

5. To go water skiing you need a boat, someone to _____ the boat, the skis and a _____ line. I think it's simpler to _____ a canoe or _____ a small sailboat.

6. When we were at the Kennedy Space Center we saw the _____ of the space shuttle.

8
Taxicabs

A taxicab, usually called a "taxi" or "cab", is an automobile that people **hire** to travel short distances. It is driven by a chauffeur, who is usually called a "driver" or more informally, "cabbie." The first American taxis appeared in 1898 and ran on electricity. By 1907, taxis and automobiles used gasoline. Today there are about 260,000 taxis operating in the United States.

In the year 1907, the taximeter was introduced. It was then that people started calling these vehicles "taxis". The meter **measures** the distance and/or time the cab has been under hire. By using the meter, drivers can measure the fare that should be charged to the passengers.

The city determines both the number of cabs in the city and the fares they can charge. Cabs usually charge a drop rate for just **getting in** the vehicle. As the taxi transports passengers to their destinations, the meter measures how far the cab has traveled and charges a fixed **rate** for each fraction of a mile. A fee may also be charged if the taxi is **stuck** in the traffic and not moving. For example, in 1992, cabs in San Francisco charged a drop rate of $1.70, and the fare increased by 30 cents for each 1/6 mile or 30 cents per minute if the cab was stuck in a traffic jam.

Taxicab companies are run in three different ways. Taxi drivers can be employees of the cab company and drive cabs owned by the company. Some companies rent the taxis to the drivers, who keep the fares for themselves. And a very few cabbies own their own cabs and work independently from any company. Drivers who work for a company keep in

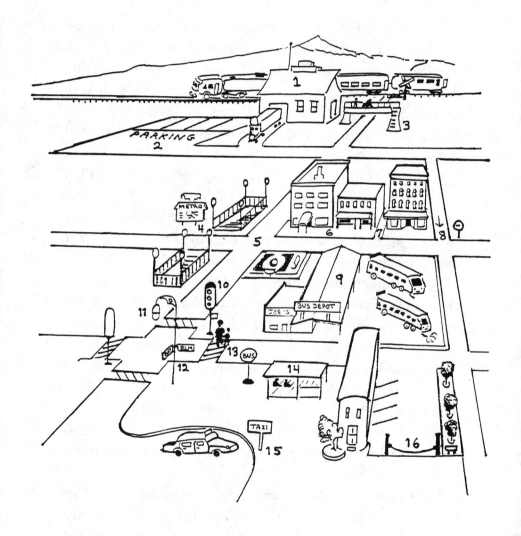

touch with the **dispatcher** by radio. The dispatcher can direct the driver to a passenger who has called for a ride.

When travelers need a taxi they can either call the taxi company or they can **catch** a taxi by waving it down in the street. Usually an empty cab travels with the taxi sign on the roof lighted. If the light is not on, the taxi is occupied. When passengers **arrive** at their destination, they pay the fare and a **tip** as they **get out**. A tip of 15 per cent is customary.

Cab drivers are **fast** drivers. They **accelerate** rapidly from stop signs and traffic lights, and they **brake** quickly when they have to stop. Often they **race** quickly through a yellow light. But cab drivers are usually safe drivers because they spend so much time practicing their trade. Passengers are safer in a taxi than they are in their own cars, especially if they do not know the city.

Some cab companies allow ridesharing, or carrying more than one passenger to similar destinations. This is especially common for trips to an airport. However, special vehicles called limousines, or limos, carry some of the passenger traffic to and from airports. The limousine, which is also the name for a long luxury automobile, is usually cheaper than a taxi.

Riding in a taxi can be a good introduction to a new city because many taxi drivers like to carry on a conversation with their passengers. Just as they are good drivers because they practice a lot, they can also be good talkers.

Key Words

hire	stuck	tip
measure	dispatcher	fast
get in	catch	accelerate
rate	arrive	brake
	get out	race

I.   Use one of the key words above in the sentences below.

1. To _____ in traffic means to be unable to move.

2. To _____ at a destination means to come to the end of a trip.

3. A _____ can be stated as dollars per mile, or miles per gallon, for example.

4. To _____ means to rent something or give a job to someone.

5. A _____ is an extra amount of money given for service.

6. _____ can mean rapid or quick.

7. To _____ can mean to move rapidly or compete to see who can go fastest.

8. To _____ means to find the dimensions, quantity or capacity of something.

9. To _____ means to increase the speed.

10. To _____ and to _____ mean to enter and leave an automobile or truck.

11. To _____ means to use the _____s to slow down or come to a stop.

12. To _____ a ride means to get or obtain a ride.

13. A _____ sends vehicles to places. Sometimes he or she may _____ the vehicle by radio.

44

II. Circle the correct form of the key word.

1. To come to a gradual stop, apply the (braker, **brakes**, braking) slowly.

2. Our (arrive, arrived, **arrival**) time is six o'clock.

3. We were late because we were (**stuck**, sticking) in a traffic jam for an hour.

4. I (tip, tipping, **tipped**) him only a dollar because I thought he drove too (**fast**, faster, fastest).

5. They drove at a high (**rate**, rating, rated) of speed throughout the night.

6. I (catch, **caught**, catching) a ride home last night with my friend.

7. The company has (hire, **hired**, hiring) a new chauffeur.

8. Deceleration is the opposite of (accelerate, accelerated **acceleration**).

9. We will (**dispatch**, dispatched, dispatcher) a cab immediately.

10. I'm late because I (get, **got**, gotten) out at the wrong corner.

11. Who won the (**race**, racing, raced) last night?

12. A kilometer is a unit of (measuring, measured, **measurement**).

III. In the paragraph below, the wrong key words are in the blanks. Cross out the wrong words and write in the correct ones.

A cab ~~accelerated~~ *braked* to a sudden stop in front of me. I watched as a big man who ~~tipped~~ *raced* at least two meters ~~got~~ *tipped* ~~in~~, paid the fare, and ~~measured~~ *got in* the driver. The cab ~~braked~~ *accelerated* rapidly and disappeared into the night. I walked up to him.

"Sorry I'm late," he said . " Got here as as ~~raced~~ *measured* as I could."

"Better late than never," I said.

"I almost didn't make it, but I managed to ~~hire~~ *hire* the last flight out of Shanghai."

45

"So what happened? Didn't you _catch_ on time?"

"Yeah, we were on time, and I was able to _arrive_ a cab right away. As I _got_ _out_ the taxi, I told the driver to step on the _dispatcher_."

"So how come you're late? Get _fast_ in traffic?"

"As a matter of fact, we did. Fortunately, the cabbie radioed to the _accelerator_ who told him the Southeast Expressway was clear. So he _stuck_ across town and then came down the Expressway."

IV. Use the correct form of one of the key words in each of the sentences below.

1. Hundreds of vehicles were _____ in the heavy snow.

2. In the very first _____, the horse I bet on won.

3. This car can _____ from 0 to 60 m.p.h. in seven seconds. That is really _____!

4. As soon as he got off the plane, he _____ _____ a limo.

5. Instead of stepping on the _____, he stepped on the _____ and crashed into the car ahead of him.

6. The service here is terrible. I'm not going to leave a _____.

7. Instead of taking me to the departure area, she took me to the _____ area.

8. She _____ _____ of the taxi and got on a bus.

9. Our company has _____ a bus for a trip to Fenway Park.

10. Can I _____ a ride with you tomorrow? My wife needs the car.

11. At this ____, the tropical rain forest will be destroyed in just a few years.

12. The _____ of this room are 10x8x6 meters.

13. The _____ sent every available police car to the scene of the crime.

9
International Airlines

The first person to fly solo across the Atlantic Ocean was Charles Lindbergh. When he landed in Paris after the 3,610-mile flight from Long Island, New York, to Paris, France, in 1927, he instantly became an American hero. His plane, the "Spirit of St. Louis," is on exhibit today in the National Air and Space Museum in Washington, D.C. Lindbergh's flight took 33½ hours. Amelia Earhart, another national hero, was the first woman to make a solo transatlantic flight. She flew from Newfoundland, Canada, to Ireland in 1932. The 2,026 mile flight took her almost 15 hours. Today, a transatlantic flight takes only 6-7 hours in a modern jet aircraft.

The United States has 17 of the world's 25 busiest international airports. A huge international airport such as New York's JFK, Heathrow in London or Frankfurt in Germany are exciting places. Aircraft of all types and from every national airline are **landing** and **taking off** in a steady **stream**. At the check-in counters, along the concourses and in the departure lounges people from everywhere are arriving, walking, waiting and departing. Almost any language can be heard in the passenger lounges, but in the **control** tower, the air traffic controllers direct this incredible **flow** of aircraft traffic in English, the language of international air travel.

Making an international flight requires more preparation than a domestic flight. When people travel abroad for the

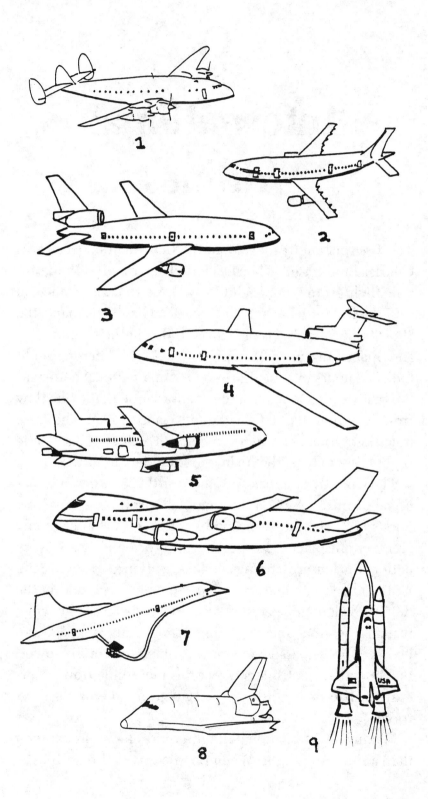

1

2

3

4

5

6

7

8

9

first time, they must first obtain a passport. For many travelers, a visa will be required in order to enter a foreign country. Visas allow a country to control the number of visitors, and their purpose.

Travelers making an international flight are asked to be at the airport at least 90 minutes before the plane is **scheduled** to depart. Because international flights **accommodate** many people, it takes a long time for all the passengers to check in, check their luggage, and get their seat assignments.

When passengers arrive and disembark in the foreign country, they must pass through immigration and customs before they are allowed to enter the country. Officials check the passport and visa to be sure everything is correct. At the customs desk, customs officers may **inspect** their luggage. Travelers are asked to **declare** what they are bringing into the country. Limited amounts of items such as tobacco and alcohol may be brought in **duty**-free. Items over the specified limit are taxed, and the traveler has to pay a duty tax.

Due to the increase in terrorist **hijackings** and bombings, airports around the world are tightening their **security**. Sometimes travelers are asked questions about their luggage: Who **packed** it, and where has it been since it was packed?

In spite of terrorism, air travel is still the safest method of travel. Between 1986 and 1988, for example, the average fatality rate for scheduled airlines was 0.03 fatalities per 100 million passenger miles. For passenger trains it was 0.06, for buses it was 0.03 and for automobiles and taxis it was 1.23. Anyone can drive a car, but it takes years of training before a **pilot** can fly for a scheduled airline.

Key Words

land	schedule	hijack
take off	accommodate	security
stream	inspect	pack
control	declare	pilot
flow	duty	

I. Use the key words above in these sentences.

1. When you arrive at customs, you have to _____ what you are bringing in.

2. You do not pay tax on items purchased in a _____- free shop.

3. An official may want to _____ your suitcases.

4. Airlines are working very hard to provide _____ for passengers.

5. When a plane arrives, it _____s. When it leaves, it _____s _____.

6. After the arrival, a steady _____ of passengers left the plane.

7. We are on _____, so we should land on time.

8. The _____ of arriving and departing aircraft is heaviest in the morning and in the evening.

9. The old DC-3s could _____ only 21 passengers.

10. To _____ means to direct or regulate.

11. The terrorists attempted to _____ the plane.

12. Although one of the engines was not working, the _____ made a safe landing.

13. I hate to _____ and un_____ suitcases.

II. Choose the correct form of the word.

1. (schedule, scheduled, scheduling) We are now operating on our winter _____.

2. (pack, packed, packing) Did you _____ your own luggage?

3 (secure, security) You should now pass through _____ control.

4. (inspect, inspected, inspection) Please have your bags open and ready for _____.

5. (declare, declared, declaration) Please fill out this customs _____ form.

6. (land, landed, landing) We will be _____ in five minutes.

7. (pilot, piloted, piloting) He has been _____ 747s for years.

8. (flow, flowed, flowing) The traffic is _____ smoothly today.

9. (accommodate, accommodations) We will provide free _____ at the airport hotel.

10. (take off, took off, taking off) Yesterday we _____ in the morning.

11. (stream, streamed, streaming) Passengers from everywhere are _____ out the doors.

12. (control, controlled, controlling) Is it necessary to _____ the movement of people across international borders?

13. (control, controllers, controlling) Air traffic _____ at international airports must speak English.

III. Use these clues to complete the puzzle.

ACROSS

1. a place to stay
7. _____pack (take out)
8. put in a bag
9. timetable
12. no cost
13. _____pack (pack again)
14. Japan Air Lines
15. _____stop
16. secure
18. arrive _____ a place
21. Korean Air Lines
23. take _____
26. go and come back (abbreviation)
27. arrival
29. where planes fly
30. flow
31. journey

DOWN

2. to direct or regulate
3. _____ time (not late)
4. say, state
5. look at closely
6. _____ way or round
   trip ?
10. steal a plane
11. stopover
17. moves
19. trip in the air
20. arrives
22. door at an airport
24. travel by air
25. _____safe (dangerous)
28. check- _____

IV. Use the correct form of the key words in these sentences.

1. I'm sorry, but you'll have to pay _____ on those bottles of wine. And by the way, you should have _____ them.

2. Please fasten your seat belts and prepare for _____.

3. This little boat here will _____ four people.

4. This is your _____ speaking. I'm sorry, but we will be making an <u>un</u>_____ landing in Atlantis. We have been _____.

5. This idea of yours will never _____ _____. It just won't fly, JP.

6. My car didn't pass the safety _____. I need new brakes.

7. Many young travelers like to use a back _____ instead of a suitcase.

8. The Gulf _____ is an ocean current, and the jet _____ is an air current.

9. This is a maximum _____ prison. It's impossible to get out.

10. A lot of people are working very hard to _____ the _____ of drugs across national borders.

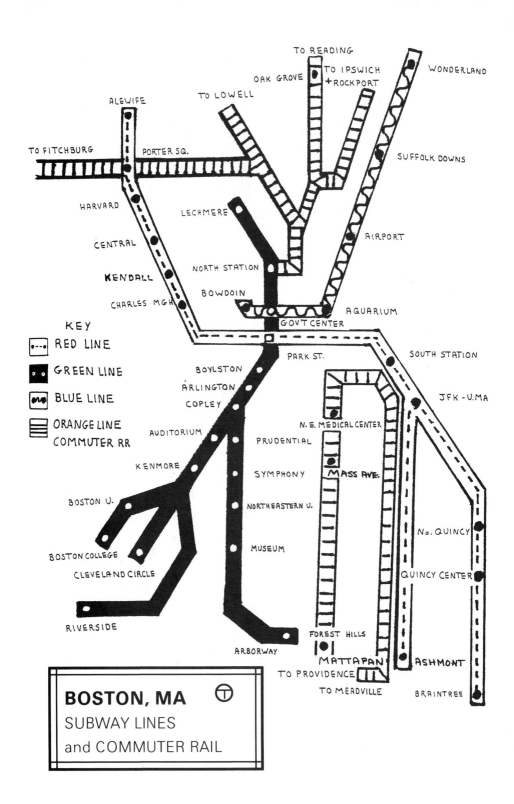

10
Subways

Subways are underground trains that are used in cities where there is not enough room for above-ground trains. Subways transport large numbers of people into and out of city centers through underground **tunnels** without interfering with the **surface** traffic.

The first subway opened in 1863 in London. It used a steam-driven **locomotive** to pull the cars. America's first subway opened in Boston in 1897. New York City's subway, opened in 1904, is today the largest subway **system** in the world, with 232 miles of track and 462 stations.

Large systems often have several lines. The lines are often given color names, such as "the green line." At **transfer** stations, passengers can transfer from one line to another.

The first completely automatic subway system opened in 1976 in the San Francisco Bay Area. The modern cars offer a **smooth**, fast ride. The cars have operators, but they usually only monitor the train's speed and operate the doors.

Some subways charge the same fare no matter what distance is traveled. These systems use **tokens** that passengers deposit into a **turnstile** as they enter the station. Other systems charge various fares. This type of system requires special tickets that measure the distance the rider has traveled. Passengers must purchase a ticket to enter the subway. These tickets can have any value the traveler wishes, but travelers must buy a ticket that is worth at least a **one-way** fare to their destination.

To enter the subway, the traveler puts the ticket into a slot at the front of the turnstile. A computer inside the turnstile records on the ticket what station the traveler has entered. Then the ticket comes out another slot, and when the traveler removes it, the turnstile opens.

After travelers pass through the turnstile, they descend a staircase or escalator to the train platform. When the train **pulls into** the station, signs will **flash** on and off to show what route the train is traveling so passengers will know which train to take. When they enter the cars, they can usually find a seat unless they are traveling during **rush hour**, when there are many commuters riding the subway. Some seats near the door are usually **reserved** for older people or people with mobility problems. It is common courtesy in a subway for younger people to give their seats to older passengers when there are no other places to sit.

When the trip is completed, the traveler again puts the ticket into a slot at the front of the turnstile, but this time the computer deducts the fare from the value of the ticket. If the value is sufficient, the turnstile opens.

Cable cars and trolleys, or streetcars, are a cross between subways and buses. They operate on the surface on tracks, but they usually have only one car and they make frequent stops. Today the cable cars of San Francisco and the street-cars of New Orleans are tourist attractions, as well as **transit** systems.

Key Words

tunnel	transfer	**pull in**	**one-way**
surface	smooth	**flash**	**transit**
locomotive	token	**rush hour**	
system	turnstile	**reserved**	

I.   The key words above are defined or explained below. Write the correct key word at the beginning of each sentence.

1. _____ : Half of a round-trip journey.

2. _____ : A road or railway that goes under the ground.

3. _____ : A coin that is used to operate a turnstile.

4. _____ : To turn something on and off quickly several times.

5. _____ : The top or outer part of something.

6. _____ : Quiet and steady, without interruption or uncomfortable movements.

7. _____ : The busy part of the day when commuters are coming from or going to work and the traffic is heavy.

8. _____ : A number of things working together as part of a whole.

9. _____ : The part of a train that has an engine and pulls the cars.

10. _____ : To move or change from one place to another.

11. _____ : Similar in meaning to transportation or transfer; movement from one place to another.

12. _____ : Held or saved for special use, for example, a table in a restaurant.

13. _____ : To arrive. Used especially for trains and buses.

14. _____ : A kind of gate that travelers move through one at a time.

II. Circle the correct form of the word.

1. There were no problems; everything went (smooth, smoothly).

2. Hurry up! The train (is pulling in, pulls in) now.

3. Slow down when you see a (flashed, flashing) yellow light.

4. In New York we had to (transfer, transferred) from JFK to Laguardia airport.

5. This space is (reserving, reserved) for handicapped people.

6. She is very (systematic, system). She always works carefully and methodically.

7. She called the travel agency and made (reserves, reservations) for tomorrow's flight.

8. The city bus company is called the Municipal (Transit, Transition) Authority.

9. The process of making a change can be called a (transition, transit). In an airport a place where passengers wait while changing planes is called a (transit, transportation) lounge.

10. They have been (tunneled, tunneling) under the river for two years now, and the project should be completed next month.

11. When a train arrives it (pulls in, pulled in); when it departs it pulls (out, up).

III. Use the key words in the passage below.

I can still remember my first ride on the "T," which is the short name for the Metropolitan _____ Authority. At the Kenmore Square Station my mother let me put my own _____ in the _____. Then we left the bright, cheerful _____ and went down into the mysterious subway _____ to wait. Soon a light started _____, and I could see the one-eyed monster coming toward us from the deep, dark _____. Then the train _____. I was surprised that there was no _____. "But how does it go?" I asked. My mother explained that it ran on electricity like my toy _____, and she told me about the dangerous third rail that was instant death to anyone who touched it.

The doors opened, we stepped in and the train _____ _____ into the darkness. I remember it wasn't a very _____ ride. But how exciting, as we swayed and bounced noisily under the city with the lighted windows of the other trains _____ by us on the other track. It must have been during _____ _____ because I remember the car was very crowded.

Finally we slowed and _____ into Park Street Station where we _____ to the Red Line for the ride under the Charles River to Harvard Square.

IV. Use the key words in the sentences below.

1. In many countries _____ are used to operate public telephones.

2. I was embarrassed to find myself driving the wrong way on a _____ _____ street.

3. The bus for Jacksonville is just _____ _____ now.

4. You can sit anywhere. These seats are not _____.

5. During the morning _____ _____, the Mathews Bridge is _____ _____ only, into the city.

6. All _____ passengers who are _____ to another flight will be taken to the _____ lounge.

7. The "Chunnel" is a _____ that goes under the English Channel.

8. The _____ of the road was _____ and even.

9. The _____ green light means the plane is ready for boarding.

10. The 42,500-mile Interstate Highway _____ serves 90 percent of American cities having a population of 50,000 or more.

1

2

3

4

5

6

7

8

9

10

11
Trucks

The first vehicle that was used just to transport **commercial** cargo was introduced in 1900. In the United States and Canada these vehicles are called trucks. In Great Britain they are called lorries. Trucks very quickly began to take business away from the railroad industry, and by 1916 there were 250,000 trucks operating in the United States. Because the condition of the roads was not very good at that time, these trucks were used mostly for **local** transportation.

Today, trucks are a common sight on the modern highway. Trucks **deliver** more commercial goods than any other means of transportation. Trains, while less expensive than trucks, can only travel along train tracks. However, there are many more miles of road in the United States than there are of railroad tracks. A truck, therefore, can deliver its cargo to almost any address in the country. Trucks are also required for other methods of shipping. A train's cargo must be **conveyed** to the railroad station by truck, and when the train reaches its destination, the cargo must be hauled away by truck.

Trucking is not always the most economical method of shipping because only a small cargo can be shipped in a single truck. The labor required to **load** and unload the cargo and drive the truck, along with gasoline and vehicle costs, contribute to the higher cost of shipping. Trucks are most **efficient** for transporting loads on short trips of less than a few hundred miles.

Trucks are divided into three classifications: light, medium and heavy. Light trucks include vans and pickup trucks.

These vehicles are used by people making local deliveries and by those in service industries like the phone company and appliance **repairs**. They are also popular with private citizens who do a lot of hauling, like farmers.

Medium weight trucks include armored cars, dump trucks, flatbeds, liquid tank trucks, and **wreckers**. Armored cars deliver money to and from the bank. Dump trucks are essential to construction workers for hauling gravel and sand. Flatbeds are simply trucks with a flat cargo space that is not enclosed. These trucks can be used to haul machinery, lumber and construction supplies. Liquid tank trucks often carry petroleum products, but they are also used to carry products such as milk or paint. Wreckers, also called tow trucks, carry away damaged vehicles that have been in a **collision**, or vehicles that are in need of repair.

Tractor-trailer trucks, also known as 18-wheelers or semis, are classified as heavy trucks, weighing up to 20 tons. These are the trucks that do most of the long-distance cargo hauling in the trucking industry. The tractor part of a tractor-trailer houses the engine and includes a cab, where the driver operates the truck. Some cabs are large enough to include a sleeping area behind the driver's seat. The trailer can be separated from the tractor, and it is where the cargo is stored.

The tractor has three **axles**: the front axle has one wheel on each side, and the two rear axles have two wheels each on each side. On each wheel there is a large, rubber **tire**. The trailer has two axles in the rear with two wheels on each side. This is why tractor-trailers are often called 18-wheelers. When disconnected from a tractor, the trailer has two metal columns that can be lowered from the front end to keep it level.

The trucking industry has benefited greatly from the development of the Interstate Highway System. On some of these highways there are almost as many trucks as passenger cars.

Key Words

commercial	load	collision	tire
local	efficient	tractor	
deliver	repair	trailer	
convey	wrecker	axle	

I. Complete the sentences below with one of the key words above.

1. A _____ pulls a trailer. It is also the name of a vehicle used by a farmer to pull farm machinery.

2. A _____ follows or is pulled by a _____. Some _____s are used as mobile homes.

3. At each end of an _____ there is a wheel, and on each wheel there is a _____.

4. The opposite of long-distance is _____.

5. When something is broken or won't operate, we need to _____ or fix it.

6. To put cargo on a truck, we _____ it. To take it off we un_____ it. The cargo itself can be called a _____.

7. To be involved in the buying and selling of goods or services for a profit is to be involved in _____ activity.

8. An _____ operation involves a minimum effort for a maximum result.

9. A vehicle that is badly damaged or destroyed is towed away by a _____. The damaged vehicle is called a _____. It has been involved in an accident or a _____. An accident may involve only one vehicle whereas a _____ involves two or more vehicles.

10. C_____ and d_____ have similar meanings. C_____ usually means just to carry, whereas _____ means to carry and give to.

II. Choose the correct form of the key word.

1. (repair, repaired) I took my car to a _____ shop to have it _____.

2. (commerce, commercial) A _____ vehicle is used in trade, whereas a private passenger car is not involved in _____.

3. (local, locate) To _____ means to find the position or place of something.

4. (efficient, efficiently, efficiency) Is this method _____? I mean, does it operate _____? To make a profit, we must have maximum _____.

5. (collision, collided) This vehicle has been in a _____. I wonder what it _____ with?

6. (loaded, reload, unload) This vehicle has not been _____ properly. You'll have to _____ everything and then _____ it more carefully.

7. (delivered, delivery) (loading, load) The _____ truck just _____ a _____ of automobile parts.

8. (wreck, wreckage) There was a major train _____ in India. Some people are still trapped in the _____.

9. (conveys, conveyer) (load, loaders, loading) At an airport a _____ belt _____ checked luggage to the baggage _____ area. Baggage _____ then put it on the plane.

III. Unscramble these headlines and put them in the proper order.

1. **JUNGLE OF WRECKAGE LOCATED IN AIRLINER**

_____

2. **MAN IN LOCAL COLLISION INJURED**

_____

3. **AXLE BREAKS TRAILER TRACTOR ON STREET MAIN**

_____

64

4. STRIKING SHIPS TO REFUSE WORKERS LOAD

_____

5. REPAIRS TOWED FOR SUBMARINE INTO PORT

_____

6. TIRE FLAT CAUSED BY ACCIDENT

_____

7. TOMORROW COMMERCE OF CHAMBER MEETS

_____

8. EFFICIENCY OF STUDY RESULTS ANNOUNCED

_____

9. ICY ROADS OVERTURNS ON VAN DELIVERY

_____

10. VISITING MESSAGE CONVEYS RUSSIAN PEACE

_____

IV. Use the correct form of one of the key words in the sentences below.

1. There are five _____ and eighteen _____ on an eighteen-wheeler.

2. The driver sits in the _____, and the _____ is carried in the _____.

3. The mailman usually _____ the mail at 10. In fact, here comes his _____ van now.

4. We'll never be able to _____ the damage that has been done.

5. The latest jet aircraft are much more fuel-_____.

6. We wanted to have a picnic, but unfortunately the weather _____ our plans.

7. A freighter and a ferry _____ in the North Sea.

8. The _____ train stops at every station.

9. Please _____ my greetings to your director.

10. She was a military pilot before she got her _____ pilot's license.

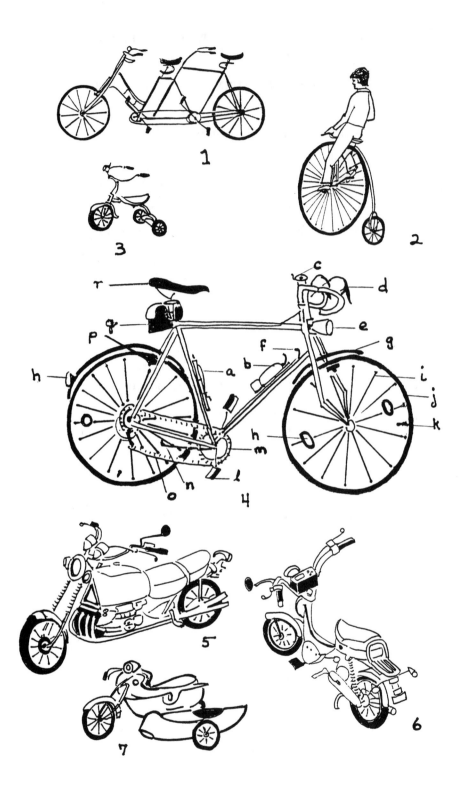

12
Bicycles and Motorcycles

Bicycles are extremely popular in America, but they are used more for sport than for transportation. For teenagers without driver's **licenses**, however, they are an essential means of **getting around** town. As a sport, biking is very widespread.

Over 100 million Americans ride bicycles at least occasionally. Many different kinds of bicycles allow people of all ages to enjoy this sport. Tricycles allow small children to get around. Larger tricycles, built like bicycles, enable elderly people to ride safely. Tandem bicycles, or bicycles built for two, let two people sit on the same bicycle. Each rider has handlebars for the hands and **pedals** for the feet but only the front handlebars actually **steer** the bike.

Daisy, Daisy,
Give me your answer, do!
I'm half crazy,
All for the Love of you!
It won't be a stylish marriage,
I can't afford a carriage,
But you'll look sweet
upon the seat
of a bicycle built for two.

Harry Dacre: *Daisy Bell*

Many people looking for an enjoyable form of exercise have become biking enthusiasts. This boom in the cycling industry has created technologically modern bicycles that help the rider move faster and farther than ever. For example, **touring** bikes, for traveling long distances on **paved** roads, have become very lightweight and use better **gear** systems. Using a ten-speed system, a rider can **shift** down to low gear while going up a hill, or shift to the highest gear when traveling fast over a flat, smooth road.

Today, many cities are trying to cut back on automobile traffic by taking advantage of the fact that many people enjoy bicycling. Thirty bikes can travel in the street space required by one car, and 18 bicycles can be **parked** in the space required for one car. In addition to saving space, bikes also do not create pollution or consume valuable oil resources. In New York City, there are now 100,000 regular biking commuters. Many towns and cities have reserved special **lanes** or paths on the streets for bicyclists.

Motorcycles are essentially motorized bicycles. Invented in Germany in 1885, motorcycles are now owned and operated by five and a half million Americans. Police officers use motorcycles to help control traffic because of their speed and the ease with which they are **maneuvered** through traffic.

Motorcycles are not operated like a car. The **throttle**, which would be the gas pedal in a car, is operated by twisting the hand grips, and a lever on the left handle controls the **clutch**. The front break is controlled by a lever on the right handle, and the rear brake is controlled by a foot pedal. Another foot pedal operates the gear shift. Because a motorcycle is a completely different vehicle from a car, motorcyclists are required to pass a driving test in order to obtain a special motorcycle license.

Motorcycles are easier to store than cars, require less **maintenance** or service and are much more energy efficient, running more than 50 miles on one gallon of gasoline. The average motorcycle weighs between 235 and 500 pounds and travels up to 80 miles per hour. Touring motorcycles, which are intended for long-distance use, are heavier and provide additional equipment like storage spaces and a windshield. Offroad motorcycles, called trail bikes or dirt bikes, are lighter and slower than the standard motorcycle and have wider tires for added traction. These bikes are used in moto-cross racing, where cyclists race across courses that include jumps, hills, and other obstacles.

Smaller versions of motorcycles include scooters and mopeds. A scooter has small wheels and a moped looks like a bicycle with a motor.

Many people enjoy the versatility and freedom of bicycles, motorcycles, mopeds, and scooters. However, in the event of an accident, they are more dangerous then cars. As a result, some states now require motorcyclists to wear helmets and goggles. In the rain these vehicles do not brake as well as cars and generally are not as visible to other drivers. While these vehicles are energy efficient, easy to store, and fun to ride, they should at all times be operated with **caution** and careful attention to safety.

Key words

license	gear	paved	get around
pedal	shift	throttle	maneuver
steer	park	clutch	maintenance
tour	lane	caution	

I. Match the following definitions and words.

1. A permit to operate
   a vehicle

2. A path; a way;
   part of a road

3. A pleasure trip

☼ ☼ ☼ ☼ ☼ ☼

4. Careful

5. Repairing and servicing a
   piece of equipment

6. The hard surface of a road

7. Not moving; stationary

☼ ☼ ☼ ☼ ☼ ☼

8. To move from place
   to place

9. To move from one gear
   to another

10. To move skillfully

☼ ☼ ☼ ☼ ☼ ☼

11. It is used by the foot

12. It brings the gears
    together

13. It changes the speed

14. It controls the supply of
    fuel to the engine

15. It controls the direction
    of a car, truck or bus

1. ___
2. ___
3. ___

4. ___
5. ___

6. ___
7. ___

8. ___

9. ___

10. ___

11. ___
12. ___

13. ___
14. ___

15. ___

a. a license
b. a tour
c. a lane

a. parked
b. cautious
c. pavement
d. maintaining

a. to shift
b. to maneuver
c. to get around

a. clutch
b. a steering wheel
c. a gear
d. a pedal
e. a throttle

70

II. Choose the correct form of the key word.

1. When I was in Bermuda, I (get, got) around with a moped.

2. (Pedaling, Pedaled) a bicycle is good exercise.

3. When he got a flat tire, he (steers, steered) to the side of the road.

4. More than a million (touring, tourists) came here last year.

5. From here the (paving, pavement) ends and the road is (unpaved, paved) for the next 10 kilometers.

6. I always have trouble (shifting, shifted) this car into reverse.

7. Let's (park, parking) the car in a (park, parking) garage.

8. The traffic was so heavy I had difficulty (maneuver, maneuvering).

9. This car has been very well (maintaining, maintained).

10. Drive (cautious, cautiously) when the pavement is wet.

III. One or more of the words in the following sentences is a nonsense word or an incorrect word that can be respelled as a key word. Write the terccor yek words at the ends of the sentences. _____ __

1. If you drink while driving you can lose your silence. _____

2. If you'll reset the car, I'll push. _____

3. I'd like to rout England this year. _____

4. Trucks are prohibited from the passing nale. _____

5. Do you remember where we karped the car? _____

6. I can't fisht my bike into low rage. _____ _____

7. There's a vaped bicycle path through the city karp.

_____ _____

8. Do you work in the incametenna department? _____

9. Green means go, red means stop, and yellow means auction. _____

10. The trothlet on a motorcycle is like the gas ledap on a car.

_____ _____

11. Do you know the song "Don't teg ourand much anymore?"

_____ _____

71

12. First, depress the chuclt delpa, and then move the stick thifs into first gare. _____ _____ _____ _____

13. Now, without looking back, spell revaumen correctly: _____

IV. Use one of the key words in the blanks in these sentences. Some of them are used twice.

1. There's a four-_____ highway from here to Alliance.

2. When you _____ the car, it's a good idea to leave it in _____.

3. It's easy to _____ _____ in this town because we have lots of bicycle paths.

4. We have decided to _____ the Maritime Provinces this year.

5. From this corner, there's a short cut to town, but it isn't _____.

6. I need to take the car in for _____ because the clutch _____ is sticking.

7. "You're not James Bond. You don't have a _____ to kill," said the angry policeman to the drunken driver.

8. The motorcycle gang roared through the town with their _____ wide open.

9. I can only drive an automatic _____ because I don't know how to use the _____ pedal.

10. Did he really _____ his bicycle the whole length of California in ten days?

11. She _____ skillfully through the downtown traffic.

12. The cause of most accidents is the nut behind the _____ wheel.

13. Let's move slowly and _____ here.

13
Moving for Fun

In the 19th century, the settlers of North America moved across the continent with a portable house called the covered wagon. It was a simple, four-wheeled vehicle pulled by a team of horses. With the invention of the motor car, the house on wheels became known as a trailer, an inexpensive house that can be pulled from one place to another. By the middle of the 20th century, nearly every town had a trailer park, which is a community of transient people who can easily move from one place to another to find work.

Nowadays on the highways of North America, there are thousands of portable houses. These vehicles have many different names and shapes. Some are pulled like trailers, and some are like small buses. But they are generally called RVs—recreational vehicles. Tourists and retired people drive their RVs around the country enjoying the freedom of the highway and the comfort of home.

Moving for recreation can also be as simple as using our legs. Some people like to **hike** along trails in parks and woods and in the mountains. Some people like to **climb** mountains. In winter, people use their legs to **ski** down snow-covered mountains or **skate** on ice. Skating can also be done on city sidewalks with roller skates and skateboards. On water, people use their legs with skis and boards to **skim** along the surface on water skis, sailboards, and surfboards.

For those who like to ride, there is **sliding** downhill on a sled or **bouncing** across snow-covered fields in a snowmobile. On the water, people operate boats of all sizes and shapes.

In the air, flying is a sport for many people. There is also a special kind of plane called the **glider**, which is a plane without an engine. This sport is also called **soaring** because the silent flight of the plane resembles the soaring flight of eagles. Some thrill-seekers enjoy soaring with a hang glider, which is simply a big kite. And for those who like the thrill of falling, there is sky**diving** with a parachute, or bungee jumping — leaping into space tied to an elastic cord.

And then there is racing. There are foot races of every kind, from the 100-meter **dash** to the 26-mile marathon. People race with all kinds of vehicles, from roller skates and bicycles to high-powered speed boats and racing cars. They also race with horses, or they go to the horse races to enjoy the thrill of the race and the thrill of gambling.

Finally, there is moving with music. There are parades in which people **march** along to the music of a band, and there is **dancing**— **swaying** with a partner to romantic music, **swinging** a partner to country music, and of course, rocking and rolling with or without a partner.

Whatever the activity, people not only need to move, but they like to move. It is not surprising, then, that movement is the basis for many kinds of recreation.

Key Words

hike	slide	dash
climb	bounce	march
ski	glide	dance
skate	soar	sway
skim	dive	swing

I. Fill in the blanks with one of the key words above.

1. You can _____ on ice.

2. You can _____ a mountain.

3. You can run in a marathon or _____ for a hundred meters.

4. You can _____ like an eagle.

5. You can _____ on a sled.

6. You can _____ in a parade.

7. You can _____ down a mountain or on water.

8. You can _____ across the surface of the water.

9. You can _____ up and down on a snowmobile.

10. You can _____ through the sky or into a swimming pool.

11. You can _____ along trails.

12. You can _____ through the air in a plane.

13. You can _____ in a disco.

14. You can _____ to music or _____ a partner.

II. Use the correct form of the word.

1. (hike, hiked, hiking) Have you ever _____ on the Appalachian Trail?

2. (climb, climbed, climbing) Every year thousands of people _____ Mount Monadnock.

3. (ski, skied, skiing) Do you enjoy _____?

4. (skate, skated, skating) The place where you _____ is called a _____ rink.

5. (skim, skimmed, skimming) The speedboat _____ across the lake.

6. (slide, slid, sliding) Children love to _____.

7. (Bounce, Bounced, Bouncing) _____ a basketball is called dribbling.

8. (glide, glided, gliding) Do you know the song "He _____ through the air with the greatest of ease?"

9. (soar, soared, soaring) I love to watch eagles and hawks as they _____ high in the sky.

10. (dive, dove, diving) She _____ to the bottom of the pool and found my ring.

11. (dash, dashed, dashing) The dog was hit by a car as it was _____ across the street.

12. (march, marched, marching) We all cheered as the _____ band _____ past.

13. (dance, danced, dancing) I could have _____ all night.

14. (sways, swayed, swaying) A very tall building actually _____ in the wind.

15. (swing, swung, swinging) He _____ his bat at the ball and missed.

III. Fill in the blanks with the correct form of a key word.

      Slow sam and Swift Steve are brothers. They look alike but they don't like the same things. Sam likes to go _____ in the national park. He enjoys mountain _____ and birdwatching. He can sit silently for hours watching an eagle _____ overhead.

      Steve, however, likes the excitement of water _____. He enjoys _____ speedily across the surface of the lake, as he _____ back and forth on the tow rope behind the boat. He likes the loud noise of the boat, and in the winter Steve loves to _____ along trails on his noisy snowmobile. He also likes to go downhill skiing, whereas Sam likes to _____ silently across the snow on cross-country skis or to _____ across a frozen lake.

      Sam likes to swim slowly across a lake, but Steve prefers to _____ from a thirty foot platform into a pool or _____ down a giant water slide. At school, Sam is a long-distance runner while Steve competes in the 100-meter _____. Steve plays flute in the orchestra and Sam plays the drum in the _____ band.

      They both like _____, but Steve likes to rock and roll and Sam prefers to _____ to soft and slow music. Swift Steve loves speed and noise, slow Sam loves peace and quiet.

79

IV. Use a form of one of the key words in the sentences below.

1. If you drop a basketball, it will _____.

2. One way to get some exercise every day is to _____ the stairs, rather than take the elevator.

3. In the playground children are _____ back and forth on _____ and _____ down _____.

4. A _____ lift carries people up a mountain.

5. Before she joined the army she had never been on a ten-mile _____ or _____ in a parade.

6. A paper airplane _____ across the room and hit the teacher in the back.

7. And now it's time to swing and _____ with Sammy Kaye and his orchestra.

8. The glider went into a steep _____ almost to the ground, and then it _____ up and _____ effortlessly over the hills.

9. This plane is designed to _____ along the ground at tree-top level.

10. As I opened the door, the cat _____ out and ran across the street.

11. In ice _____ two _____ glide around the rink to music.

80

Suggestions for the Teacher

These readings and the vocabulary can be used in a great variety of ways, adapted and modified as necessary, in order to fit your teaching situation. However, for your consideration, some suggestions are outlined below. In general, the readings and their accompanying exercises may be used either for self-study out of class or for group study in class.

For Self-Study. If the students are to use this book for out-of-class self-study, and if your intention is to provide at least minimal direction and control over their use of the material, it would be a good idea to orient the students to the book and how they are to use it. This can be done in the following way.

1. Go through the first reading with the students in class. See the group-study technique for one procedure. You should point out the redundant style of the readings and encourage them to get into the habit of trying to get at the meaning of a word from the context.

2. Go through the exercises with the students. Point out that there is an answer key.

For Group Study. The basic technique and the variations described below can be used for any of the passages. You can also, to vary the procedure, do some of the passages as group study and some as self-study.

1. Refer to the table of contents and have the students look at the key words for the passage. Ask them to note which ones they think they know and which ones they're not sure of or don't know.

2. Go over the list of key words for pronunciation. You can pronounce the words and simply have the students repeat them or have the students read them aloud.

3. Option A. Have the students read the entire passage silently.

   Option B. Have the students take turns reading the passage aloud. Note any pronunciation problems and correct them after everybody has read.

Option C. You read the passage aloud while the students listen. This option can be done twice. First the students listen with their books closed; then when you read it the second time they can follow along in their books.

General Suggestions

1. Although it is best to begin with the introductory reading and proceed through the book in sequential fashion, it is not necessary to do so.

2. You can do the readings in clusters. Divide the class into three groups. Each group does a different reading and then explains its reading to the other groups, putting the key words on the board as it explains.

3. Throughout the book there are many illustrations which lend themselves to simple question and answer practice using question words: Who, When, Where, How, Why, etc.

4. Prepare a set of 3x5 index cards. Each key word is written on a card. For each reading there are usually 12-15 different words. You can use these cards for review in a number of different ways: Flash the card and have the students explain or define it. Have the students make a sentence with the word. Give the cards to the students and have a two-team quiz game.

ANSWERS

1 — Introductory Reading

I.
1. vehicle
2. fly
3. journey
4. travel
5. mobility, move
6. walk
7. carry
8. transportation

II.
1. moved
2. journeyed
3. walk
4. vehicle, carry
5. flying, flown
6. travelers
7. mobile
8. transport

2 — Walking

I.
1. rapid
2. run
3. ride
4. distance
5. cover
6. stride
7. pace
8. jog
9. trip
10. pedestrian
11. path
12. migration

II.
1. walked, rode
2. running, jogs/is jogging
3. pace
4. covered, trip
5. rapidly, path
6. cover, distance, rapidly
7. striding
8. pedestrians

III.
1. moving
2. running
3. jogging
4. walking
5. riding
6. paced
7. strode
8. covered
9. migrated
10. pedestrians
11. distance
12. rapidly
13. path
14. trip

IV.
1. distance
2. pedestrian
3. runner
4. ride
5. rapidly
6. pace
7. joggers
8. path
9. trips
10. migrate
11. stride (for) stride
12. cover

3 — Automobiles

I.
1. smog
2. toll, fine
3. driving
4. motorist, passenger
   commuter
5. accident
6. speed
7. safety, seat belt,
   traffic
8. running, running, runs

II.
1. motorists
2. toll
3. passengers, seat
4. fine, speeding
5. accidents, safely
6. smoggy
7. runs
8. traffic
9. drive
10. commutes

III.
1. motor, running
2. passengers, seat belt
3. traffic
4. commuted
5. smog
6. TOLL, MOTORISTS, TOLL
7. SPEED, SPEED
8. SAFETY, ACCIDENT
9. FINE, DRIVING

IV.
1. passenger/commuter,
   passengers/commuters, speed
2. toll, toll-free, toll-free
3. smog-free
4. traffic
5. accidental, motor, accidents
6. runs
7. safe, accident, safety, fine
8. seat belt, passengers, seats

4 — Domestic Airlines

I.
1. destination
2. flight
3. round trip
4. nonstop
5. check-in, check in
6. altitude
7. gate
8. boarding pass, board
9. flight attendant
10. disembark
11. last
12. heading

II.
1. h.
2. e.
3. k.
4. j.
5. g.
6. l.
7. a.
8. d.
9. f.
10. b.
11. c.
12. i.

III.

Flight 103, gate 32
flight
last
nonstop
destination
disembark
flight attendants
checked in
board
heading
round trip

IV.
1. check-in
2. Flight, boarding, Gate,
   boarding passes, attendant
3. flight, heading, altitude,
   flight, last, destination,
   disembark, last
4. nonstop, round trip

5 — Railroads

I.
1. depart
2. wheel
3. way
4. fare
5. link
6. roll
7. junction
8. platform
9. haul
10. line
11. freight
12. rail
13. track

II.
1. ways
2. three-wheeled
3. rails
4. rolling
5. tracks
6. hauled, line
7. links
8. Freight
9. fares
10. depart

III.
1. c. way
2. a. platform
3. b. junction
4. d. line
5. d. freight
6. a. departure
7. c. fare
8. b. track
9. e. link
10. d. roll
11. b. rail, derailed
12. a. wheel
13. c. U-Haul

IV.
1. platform
2. junction
3. fares
4. way
5. rolling
6. departure
7. line
8. link
9. hauled
10. track
11. rails, freight, wheels

6 — Buses

I.
1. get on, get off
2. picks (you) up, drops (you) off, discharges
3. terminal, stop, routes, frequent, frequently
4. chartered, chartered
5. pass, (to) pass, passes
6. storage, luggage, rack

II.
1. My luggage is at the terminal.
2. Which route shall we take?
3. This vehicle stops frequently.
4. The bus has discharged all its passengers.
5. He got on the bus.
6. She got off the bus in Dallas.
7. We picked him up at 9 a.m.
8. We dropped him off at 11 a.m.
9. Do not pass a stopped school bus.
10. Please store your packages in the overhead rack.

III. A.

Crossword

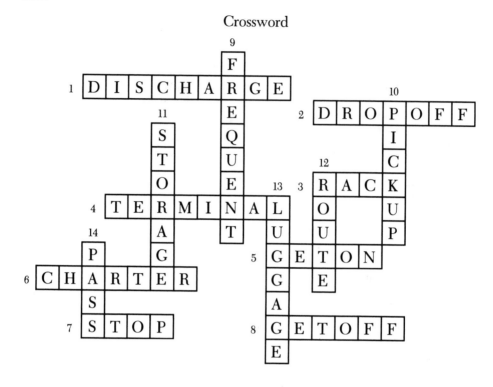

III. B.

9. FREQUENT — often
10. PICK UP — take a passenger
11. STORAGE — place to
    keep things
12. ROUTE — road, way
13. LUGGAGE — suitcases
14. PASS — go around;
    special ticket

IV.

dropping (me) off
Terminal
get on
(get) off
terminal
luggage
frequent
storage
route
stops
passed
stop
charter
discharged
picked (me) up
rack

7 — Boats

I.
1. ferry
2. paddle
3. cruise
4. port
5. cargo
6. cross
7. ship
8. launch
9. propel
10. operate
11. navigate/sail
12. tow
13. sail

II.
1. operated
2. shipment
3. crossed
4. launched
5. Navigation
6. propelled, propellers
7. cruise
8. ferry, ferried
9. paddling, paddle
10. sailing, sail
11. towed, tow

III.

port, sailing, ships,
cargoes, ships, towed,
tow, paddle, ferries,
operate, cross, ferry,
operators, navigators,
propel, launched, cruise,
port

IV.
1. cargo
2. ship
3. (air)port
4. ferried, propellers,
   cross, navigator
5. operate, tow, paddle, sail
6. launch

8 — Taxicabs

I.
1. stuck
2. arrive
3. rate
4. hire
5. tip
6. Fast
7. race
8. measure
9. accelerate
10. get in, get out
11. brake, brakes
12. catch
13. dispatcher, dispatch

II.
1. brakes
2. arrival
3. stuck
4. tipped, fast
5. rate
6. caught
7. hired
8. acceleration
9. dispatch
10. got
11. race
12. measurement

III.

braked . . . measured . . .
got out . . . tipped . . .
accelerated . . . fast . . .
catch . . . arrive . . .
hire/catch . . . got in . . .
accelerator . . . stuck . . .
dispatcher . . . raced

IV.
1. stuck
2. race
3. accelerate, fast
4. got in/into
5. brake(s), accelerator
6. tip
7. arrival
8. got out
9. hired
10. catch
11. rate
12. measurements
13. dispatcher

9 — International Airlines

I.
1. declare
2. duty
3. inspect
4. security
5. lands, takes off
6. stream
7. schedule
8. flow/stream
9. accommodate
10. control
11. hijack
12. pilot
13. pack, unpack

II.
1. schedule
2. pack
3. security
4. inspection
5. declaration
6. landing
7. piloting
8. flowing
9. accommodations
10. took off
11. streaming
12. control
13. controllers

III.

Crossword

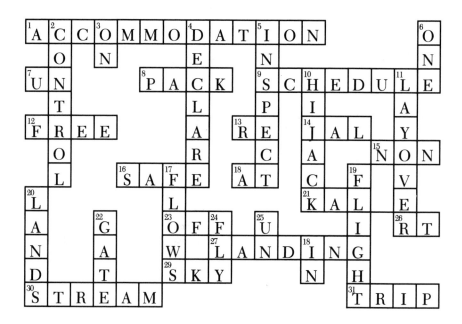

IV.
1. duty, declared
2. landing
3. accommodate
4. pilot, unscheduled
   hijacked
5. take off
6. inspection
7. backpack
8. Stream, stream
9. security
10. control, flow

10 — Subways

I.

1. one-way
2. tunnel
3. token
4. flash
5. surface
6. smooth
7. rush hour
8. system
9. locomotive
10. transfer
11. transit
12. reserved
13. pull in
14. turnstile

II.

1. smoothly
2. is pulling in
3. flashing
4. transfer
5. reserved
6. systematic
7. reservations
8. Transit
9. transition, transit
10. tunneling
11. pulls in, out

III.

Transit, token, turnstile, surface
tunnel, flashing, tunnel, pulled in
locomotive, locomotive/train,
pulled out, smooth, flashing
rush hour, pulled, transferred

IV.

1. tokens
2. one-way
3. pulling in
4. reserved
5. rush hour, one-way
6. transit/transfer, transferring, transit
7. tunnel
8. surface, smooth
9. flashing
10. System

11 — Trucks

I.

1. tractor
2. trailer, tractor, trailer(s)
3. axle, tire
4. local
5. repair
6. load, unload, load
7. commercial
8. efficient
9. wrecker, wreck, wreck/collision, collision
10. Convey, deliver, Convey, deliver

II.

1. repair, repaired
2. commercial, commerce
3. locate
4. efficient, efficiently, efficiency
5. collision, collided
6. loaded, unload, reload
7. delivery, delivered, load
8. wreck, wreckage
9. conveyor, conveys, loading, loaders

III.

1. **WRECKAGE OF AIRLINER LOCATED IN JUNGLE**
2. **LOCAL MAN INJURED IN COLLISION**
3. **TRACTOR TRAILER BREAKS AXLE ON MAIN STREET**
4. **STRIKING WORKERS REFUSE TO LOAD SHIPS**
5. **SUBMARINE TOWED INTO PORT FOR REPAIRS**
6. **ACCIDENT CAUSED BY FLAT TIRE**
7. **CHAMBER OF COMMERCE MEETS TOMORROW**
8. **RESULTS OF EFFICIENCY STUDY ANNOUNCED**
9. **DELIVERY VAN OVERTURNS ON ICY ROADS**
10. **VISITING RUSSIAN CONVEYS PEACE MESSAGE**

IV.

1. axles, tires
2. tractor, load, trailer
3. delivers, delivery
4. repair
5. efficient
6. wrecked
7. collided
8. local
9. convey
10. commercial

12 — Bicycles and Motorcycles

I.

1. a
2. c
3. b
4. b
5. d
6. c
7. a
8. c
9. a
10. b
11. d
12. a
13. c
14. e
15. b

II.

1. got
2. Pedaling
3. steered
4. tourists
5. pavement, unpaved
6. shifting
7. park, parking
8. maneuvering
9. maintained
10. cautiously

III.

1. license
2. steer
3. tour
4. lane
5. parked
6. shift, gear
7. paved, park
8. maintenance
9. caution
10. throttle, pedal
11. get around
12. clutch pedal, shift, gear
13. maneuver

IV.

1. lane
2. park, gear
3. get around
4. tour
5. paved
6. maintenance, pedal
7. license
8. throttles
9. shift, clutch
10. pedal
11. maneuvered
12. steering
13. cautiously

13 — Moving for Fun

I.

1. skate
2. climb
3. dash
4. soar
5. slide
6. march
7. ski
8. skim
9. bounce
10. dive
11. hike
12. glide
13. dance
14. sway, swing

II.

1. hiked
2. climb
3. skiing
4. skate, skating
5. skimmed
6. slide
7. Bouncing
8. glides
9. soar
10. dove
11. dashing
12. marching, marched
13. danced
14. sways
15. swung

III.

hiking, climbing, soar/soaring, skiing, skimming, swings, bounce, glide, skate, dive, slide, dash, marching, dancing, sway

IV.

1. bounce
2. climb
3. swinging, swings sliding, slides
4. ski
5. hike, marched
6. glided
7. sway
8. dive, climbed soared
9. skim
10. dashed
11. dancing, skaters

Key to Illustrations

1. Introductory Reading
page viii
1. walking and carrying
2. riding a horse
3. cart
4. sailing ship
5. steamboat
6. canoe
7. early automobile
8. steam train/railroad train
9. airplane (DC-3)

2. Walking
page 4
1. a hiker (hiking)
2. walking
3. jogging
4. trotting
5. jumping
6. running
7. wheeling (a wheelchair)
8. striding
9. crawling

3. Automobiles
page 10
1. economy car
2. luxury car
3. station wagon
4. sports car
5. convertible
6. sedan
7. taxi
8. limousine
9. van
10. racing car

4. Domastic Airlines
page 16
1. Wright Brothers' airplane —
   Flyer I
2. biplane
3. helicopter
4. floatplane
5. skiplane
6. commuter (Beechcraft)
7. light plane (Piper Cub)
8. Business jet (Lockheed Dash 8)
9. DC-9 jetliner
10. Boeing 737 jetliner

5. Railroads
page 22
1. Steam locomotives
2. passenger train
3. tank car
4. box car
5. caboose
6. Diesel locomotive
7. flatcar

6. Buses
page 28
1. double-decker (omnibus)
2. city bus
3. tour bus/intercity bus
4. shuttle bus
5. school bus

7. Boats
page 36
1. ocean liner/cruise ship
2. freighter/cargo ship
3. ferry
4. harbor pilot boat
5. sailing yacht
6. sailboat
7. tug boat
8. barge
9. fishing boat
10. speedboat
11. space capsule
12. submarine
13. underwater research
    vessel

8. Taxicabs
page 42
1. train/railroad station
2. parking lot
3. pedestrian overpass
4. subway station entrance
5. intersection
6. one block
7. alley
8. one-way street
9. bus terminal/depot
10. traffic light
11. street lamp/light
12. corner
13. pedestrian crosswalk
14. bus stop
15. taxi stand
16. dead end street

9. International Airlines

11. Trucks

12. Bicycles and Motorcycles

13. Moving for Fun

Key Word Index

The numbers after each key word are lesson numbers.

Other Vocabureaders from Pro Lingua Associates

The Zodiac: Exploring Human Qualities and Characteristics. Mary R. Moore, 1984.

Potluck: Exploring American Foods and Meals. Raymond C. Clark, 1985.

American Holidays: Exploring Traditions, Customs and Backgrounds. Barbara Klebanow and Sara Fischer, 1986.

Summer Olympic Games: Exploring International Athletic Competition. Raymond C. Clark and Michael Jerald, 1987.

Money: Exploring the Ways We Use It. Raymond C. Clark, 1989.

Vocabulary Builders

Lexicarry: An Illustrated Vocabulary Builder. Patrick R. Moran, 1990.

Getting a Fix on Vocabulary: Using Words in the News. The System of Affixation and Compounding in English. Raymond C. Clark and Janie L. Duncan, 1990.

Resource Handbooks for Language Teachers:

Language Teaching Techniques, 2nd, Revised Edition. Raymond C. Clark, 1987.

The ESL Miscellany 2nd, Revised Edition. Raymond C. Clark, Patrick R. Moran and Arthur A. Burrows, 1991.

Index Card Games For ESL. Ruthanne Brown, et al., 1992.

Families: 10 Card Games for Language Learners. Marjorie Fuchs, Jane Critchley, and Thomas Pyle, 1986.

Conversation Inspirations for ESL. Nancy Ellen Zelman, 1990.

Story Cards: The Tales of Nasreddin Hodja. Raymond C. Clark, 1991.

Technology Assisted Teaching Techniques. Janie Duncan, 1987.

Experiential Language Teaching Techniques, 2nd, Revised Edition. Michael Jerald and Raymond C. Clark, 1988.

Cultural Awareness Teaching Techniques. Jan Gaston, 1983.